THE WRITINGS OF
ST. CHRODEGANG OF METZ

Translated by: D.P. Curtin

Dalcassian Publishing Company
PHILADELPHIA, PA

THE WRITINGS OF ST. CHRODEGANG OF METZ

Copyright @ 2010 Dalcassian Publishing Company

All rights reserved. No part of this publication may be reproduced, distributed, or transmitted in any form or by any means, including photocopying, recording, or other electronic or mechanical methods, without the prior written permission of the publisher, except in the case of brief quotations embodied in critical reviews and certain other non-commercial uses permitted by copyright law. For permission request, write to Dalcassian Publishing Company at dalcassianpublishing at gmail.com

ISBN: 979-8-8691-5861-1 (Paperback)

Library of Congress Control Number:
Author: Curtin, D.P. (1985-)

Printed by Ingram Content Group, 1 Ingram Blvd, La Vergne, Tennessee

First printing edition 2010.

THE WRITINGS OF ST. CHRODEGANG OF METZ

CONFIRMATION OF PRIVLEGE

In the name of God, Chrodegang, as if I were a sinner, bishop of the city of Metenza (Metz), while in the divine volumes a series of Scriptures according to the possibility of the mediocrity of my senses, with stunned ears and diligent consideration, I looked into what the Son of God said, hearing: Give and it will be given to you (Luke 6), and elsewhere: Give alms, and behold, all things will be made clean for you (Luke 11): therefore I began to search in sorrow what I should do for the remedy of my soul, what I should do for washing away the weight of sins, or in which I should imitate the examples of the ancient Fathers, of my predecessors in the works which we believe that it pleased God; hence, by the help of God, together with the provision and will of our lord the most pious and glorious King Pippin of the Franks, and with the consent of our canonical brothers, spiritual and God-fearing lay faithful of Saint Stephen, I built a monastery in a place called Gorzia, in the village of Scarpon, in honor of the most blessed apostles Peter and St. Paul, nor St. Stephen, or the rest of the saints, and founding and endowing the monastery itself with the things and lands that had come to me by the laws due to the sales and exchanges, namely, on the condition that the

monks in the monastery according to the order and rule of our holy father the blessed abbot and they always live in perpetual times, and as it is written there, having nothing wholly their own, but let all things be common to them in all things, so that they may be able to pray both for themselves and for others; therefore, the affection of charity and love of their brethren, for their peace and order, compelled us how, with the help of God, they might be able to fulfill his rule and order, and that it should remain for us and our successors as a reward, and to set off from the right path an unshakable limit, that he might obtain eternally henceforth, propitiating God firmness, that no one should presume to take away from us new decisions on this matter, while in ancient times, according to the consideration of the pontiffs, they saw that the other monasteries subject to them were in all respects preserved and secure; therefore, for the divine insight, or for the remedy of our souls, or of our pontifical successors, together with the provision and will of the most pious and glorious King Pippin, and the consent of our brethren, it behooves us to preserve them for their rest and tranquility, and neither by us, nor by our archdeacon , nor should they be disturbed by the rest of the orderlies of St. Stephen, by any man, nor condemned, nor robbed of their property, contrary to the order of reason, but having inspected their instruments, in accordance with the constitution which we have instituted for them, should hold and possess the things themselves in quiet order, and of that which we gave and formed to the monastery itself was either given and established by God-fearing men, or something handed down as a gift, or offered on the altar, or sacred volumes, or any other species that pertains to the adornment of divine worship, have been contributed at the present time or will be contributed hereafter, not let us take it away, and I beg of the executed petition, and I demand that the lords and successors of my bishops, and the other administrators of St. Stephen's, for the sake of the name of the holy Trinity, which has been intimated above, in perpetual times to be done for their reward, preserve the very brothers who appear to be in the monastery itself, and let it be the monastery itself subject to the mandeburde and defense of the church of St. Stephen of Metz, as is contained in that instrument which we made from the monastery itself to the church of St. Stephen, that it may please them to invoke the mercy of the Lord for the life and safety of the king and the stability of the kingdom of the Franks, and for their pontiffs and their subjects; and in accordance with the divine dispensation, when the abbot had migrated from the monastery to the Lord, whom all that assembly of monks had unanimously chosen as having found the best rule and merits of life, together with the consent and will of the bishop of the city, they should have him himself as abbot, and if in the assembly itself, which is absent, if they could not find one who would govern them regularly, then the pontiff himself, with their consent and will, would choose an abbot from another monastery, as we have said above, who would preside over them regularly and according to order; let him send, except he who governs them according to order, and if the pontiff himself or any other power does otherwise, he will give an account in the divine district judgment before the eyes of God with the most blessed Peter, the chief of the apostles, and the holy protomartyr Stephen; and if the aforesaid pontiff comes to the monastery itself, when it pleases him, by prayer or by visiting the brethren, or makes some stay for the sake of winning souls, when from there he wishes to have a return in the name of God, he shall return without any earthly service required. How can monks who are called solitary, from perfect rest, or security, be able to exult in the protection of the Lord for long periods of time, and living under a holy rule for the progress of the church and the safety of the king or the country, be able to implore the mercy of the Lord more fully and more attentively? And if, which is absent, the monks themselves are found to be lukewarm or neglectful of their rule or religion, they shall be corrected by their abbot according to their rule; but if the abbot himself does not prevail, then the aforesaid pontiff must check, because nothing is taken away from the canonical authority, whatever of the pontiffs of the faith is given for quiet tranquility, so that on this account it may stand firmer with vigor. And our brethren of the congregation of St. Stephen, who were faithful to him, signed their consent.

> *Bishop Chrodegangus, the sinner, read and subscribed to this confirmation made by me.*
> *Bishop Adalfridus the sinner signed.*
> *I, subscribe to the hearing of the bishop, the sinful wolf.*
> *I, called Fulcharius, an unworthy bishop, subscribed to Rothing's advocate.*
> *Wulfrannus, the bishop called, subscribed in the name of Christ.*
>
> *Bishop Herineus signed Sigismund.*
> *I, Bishop Mangaudus, subscribed.*
> *I, Memorianus Chorchidianus subscribed.*
> *I subscribed to Deotmarus as if he were a sinful bishop.*
> *I subscribed to the mad abbot.*
> *Bishop Jacob the sinner signed.*
> *Menesbius, the sinner bishop, subscribed.*
> *I am a bold sinner bishop.*
> *Although Chardobachius was a sinful bishop, I subscribed.*
>
> *The Bishop of London subscribed.*
> *I, Lupus, though an unworthy bishop, subscribed in the name of Christ.*
> *Tedecarius the sinner bishop subscribed*
> *Fortunus the sinner bishop subscribed*
> *Sedonius subscribed as if he were a sinful bishop.*
> *Bishop Deofrid signed.*
> *Bishop Sadrius signed.*
> *I, Angilrannus, signed.*
> *Sadebert signed as if an unworthy bishop.*

Undersigned Rotelinus, Gontelmus, Brandomus, Sigibertus, Zacharias, Rachinnatus, Ego, Gonterius, Abbo, Adelelinus, Angelelinus, Sadrius.

I, Richerus, or Wasco, as if an unworthy deacon, ordered this confirmation to be reread and signed.

An act in the Compendium of the palace officially assembled in a synod in the year from the Incarnation of the Lord 756, ind. 9, epac, 15, conc. 4, in the 6th year (or 4, as others prefer) of the reign of Pippin the glorious king, under the 10th day of Cal. of June

A DIPLOMA FOR THE FOUNATION OF GORZIA

In the name of the Father, and of the Son, and of the Holy Spirit, amen. I, Chrodegang, as if unworthy, if not by work or name, bishop by the grace of God, together with the provision and will of the illustrious man Pippin, the elder of our house, our elder, and with the consent of all our peers, abbots, priests, deacons, subdeacons, or men of St. Stephen of the church of Metzen, or of those good laymen who seem to be there in the service of St. Stephen, I thought, in the case of human frailty, how, by giving to the Lord, we can wash away our sins and reach eternal joys. Therefore, we donate the belongings of St. Stephen to that basilica of St. Peter and St. Stephen, or of the rest of the saints, which we built anew, at the end of Haldiniac, in the village of Scarponinse, where Gorzia rises, and to the cell itself, which we built there, and for the work of the servants of God of the inhabitants there, by this testament, whereby those monks or the poor may have sustenance and clothing or other comfort there; this is whatever in the Haldianic end, where we built the basilica of St. Peter itself, whatever we procured or came to us by sale, gift, exchange, and whatever we obtained from the Haldianic end itself, in each part, two leuas, was either handed over to us or exchanged, or previously compared there, or, concerning any genius, it has come down to us in laws. This to the very cell already mentioned by this testament, for the increase of our wages, and whatever St. Stephen's house had there at the very end of Haldiniac, to the basilica itself, or to that cell of St. Peter, should proceed in increases. We grant also in the very village of Scarponinse, in a place called Siurone, whatever Rigoaldus delegated to the part of St. Stephen by the instrument of his charters, together with that basilica which is built in honor of St. Paul, or whatever looks to this end in Godolinovilla and Bodelocurte, or in the end of Haldiniac and in the end of Baudicia, or in the end of Aconia, or whatever in the end Rigoaldus and his brother Gontrannus delegated to the part of St.

Stephen, through their instruments, and whatever Bavo delegated in the town of Tantalinus, through his instrument, to the house of St. Stephen. We also grant, in the village of Scarponinse, in the village of Buesarias, that the house of St. Stephen seems to have there, according to the laws, or in those lands, as has already been said, which good men, through their instruments, delegated to the house of St. Stephen. We also grant in the very village of Scarpon the village of St. Stephen, whose name is Puina, with manses, courts, ortilis, houses, buildings, lands, fields, meadows, vineyards, woods, cultivated and uncultivated, waters, watercourses, mancipi, litis, or by correspondence, savings of both sexes, movable or immovable, or whatever by sale, donation, exchange, reaches the very house of St. Peter or the very cell with God's helper, may he prosper in the increase. We give to Novus Sartus half of that forest where those brothers or their men can make a madram to the very house of St. Peter. Let us also give those belongings of St. Remigius, when the basilica itself was built in Sigeus, or whatever relates to this, or which until now Adventius has held by the benefice of St. Stephen. We also give four vineyards in Sigeius with their winemakers and their wives and their servants and their lots. These are their names: Harduinus the vintner, his epistolary wife, Erlofridus the vintner, his wife Raganlindis, Erlulfus the vintner, his epistolary wife, Wandelbert the vintner, his epistolary wife. In the village itself we give the maids with the following names: Amelbergane maid, Rigobertane maid, Eminane maid and that tithe of those vineyards, both wine and food, or from elsewhere. We also give to the Castle three vineyards with winemakers and their wives and their estates or their lots; these are their names: Adelfridus the vintner, his wife a handmaid named Gaucia, Anglifridus the vintner with his wife, likewise Adelfridus with his wife a Wandelbergane handmaid and a German maid. We also give to Gaudiacum that oratory which was built in honor of St. Andrew, or whatever belongs to it, or which Teudonius held there by the benefice of St. Stephen. We also give to Cuberacus that basilica which was built in honor of St. Martin, which the chancellor Candidianus held by benefice, or whatever looks to the basilica itself, to the very house of St. Peter and to those brothers or monks, let it proceed in augmentations, and that tithe from Prunidus, from the food, of the hay, of the cows, of the swine, of the verves, or of the beasts, or from any other place, may proceed in increments to the hut itself already mentioned. We also give a tithe of Miliriacus, of that wine which will be gathered there every year. We also give the town of Cluserado above the Musella, with that village called Riviniacus, with manses, courts, orchards, houses, buildings, lands, fields, meadows, vineyards, woods, cultivated and uncultivated, waters, watercourses, mancipia , with the savings of both sexes, movable and immovable, or whatever appears to be at the very end of St. Stephen's cottage, to St. Peter's cottage itself, or to the cell itself, as has been said above, to the monks themselves, or to the brothers themselves in increments. We also give the whole tithe of that wine from Bredracul every year. All these above intimated to Gorzia itself, or to those monks, and the poor hoping for alms there, let them progress every time in increase. If indeed any one of my successors or brothers of the aforesaid clergy of Metenza (Metz), or any other person, has attempted to come against the pages of this testament of mine, or has wanted to do anything from it, without my will, has tried to lessen my devotion in all things, or has refused to fulfill the sacraments above he has disdained to observe intimates; while I do not want to curse anyone, let him not know that he will be caused by this with me on the terrible day of judgment before the tribunal of Christ; and, that at all times this page of our testament should remain unshaken, I confirmed it with my own hand, and asked our brothers or other good men who were assent to confirm it.

It was done publicly at Andernacus in the palace. In the year from the Incarnation of the Lord 745, indictment 13, agreement 14, concurrently 4, in the 6th year of King Childeric, the 20th day of May. The seal of the illustrious man of Pippin the Older.

THE RULE OF THE CANONS ACCORDING TO THE RECENSION OF LABBEI

PROLOGUE

During the times of the most pious and serene King Pippin, Chrodogang was the servant of the servants of God, bishop of the city of Metense (Metz).

If the authority of the canons of the three hundred and eighteen, and of the rest of the holy Fathers, were to last, and the clergy and the bishop lived according to their standard of rectitude, it would seem superfluous for us, the few and smallest, to retrace something on this matter so orderly arranged, and indeed say something new; but while the negligence of pastors and subjects has grown too much even in these times, what else is there for us to do, who have come to such a grave crisis, except to bring our clergy back, as much as we can, if not as much as we should, to the line of rectitude, inspiring God.

Therefore, although I had obtained the pontifical chair of this see unworthy, as soon as I had begun to supervise the care of my pastoral office, and I saw that the clergy and the people had become so negligent, I began to complain sadly, what I should do; but supported by divine help, and aided by the consolation of my spiritual brothers, I wished, compelled by necessity, to make a small decree, by which the clergy should control themselves from the unlawful, put away the vicious, and abandon the evils long and distantly usurped; so that while the mind is emptied of habitual vices, the good and best things may more easily be inserted.

For relying on the sacred Scriptures, we decree that all should be of one accord in the divine offices and in the sacred lessons, and in obedience to their bishop and superiors, as the canonical order demands, prepared, connected with charity, fervent zeal for good, united in love, from disputes, or scandals, or hatred, apart. Whosoever may be their shepherd, he shall take care not only of the carnal, but also of the spiritual, and in both respects he shall have the most shrewd concern, in which he has the opportunity, that he may repress vices, and hasten to cut them off at the root, as they have begun to arise, so that they may prevail; and what is necessary for human uses, according to the form arranged below, he dares to provide them. That when Christ, the shepherd of the shepherds and judge of the living and the dead, will sit in the seat of his majesty on the last and terrible day, he will sit with all the nations, and all the clergy will see him with a revealed face, and if not with the chief shepherds and the flocks committed to him for the dispensation of talents and multiplied spiritual gains we deserve to hear: Blessed, good and faithful servant (Matt. 25), or at least this is granted, so that the forgiveness of sins is given in full. Since it is clear to whom the forgiveness of sins is granted in full, entrance into the kingdom is not denied; for neither can he be judged unhappy, who happens to have any part in paradise. But there the lot is given to those who, as far as they are able, by the merit of life, to this end, in the course of this time, while it is permitted, hasten to run.

Let us therefore concentrate our attention on this as much as we can, because we cannot do as much as we ought; and let our life be bitter for a time in penitence, lest the divine vengeance, which is now gentle and awaits, afterwards rages for vengeance.

CHAPTER I.-- *On humility*

The divine Scripture cries out to us: Everyone who exalts himself will be humbled; and whoever humbles himself will be exalted (Luke 14). And the humbler you are, the greater the height of glory follows you (James 4). And because God resists the proud but gives grace to the humble (Pro. 16). Everyone who is arrogant is unclean before the Lord; for when you see anyone proud, you do not doubt that he is the son of the devil; and whom thou hast seen humble, thou must absolutely believe that he is the son of God. For we have glimpsed a few of many things, in order to provoke your hearts to the love of humility, and to withdraw from pride, which is detestable and inimical to God. For while all the human race of Christians, and all the common people agree to have humility, it is extremely unjust, worst, and detestable that those who have united themselves more particularly to the service of God should abandon humility, and associate themselves with pride, or diabolical tyranny. For this reason it is necessary that he who has hitherto lived with a proud and exalted countenance, at the persuasion of the devil, should arise before, with the help of God, through humility and charity, or obedience, or through the other good precepts of God, because it is much better to reign with Christ in the heavenly places through humility than I was drowned with the devil through pride in hell with the rest of the despisers.

CHAPTER II.-- *On the order of the congregation of canons.*

Let the canons preserve their orders in such a way that they are ordered in their degrees according to the legitimate institution of the Roman Church, in all places, that is, in the church, or wherever they have conjoined themselves at the same time, and reason warrants it; with the exception of those whom the bishop has established in a higher degree, or has degraded, for certain reasons; let all the rest, as we have said, keep their ranks as they are ordered. Therefore, the younger ones should honor their elders, and the older ones should love their younger ones in God.

But in the appeal of his name no one is permitted to call another by his pure name, but, according to the constitution of the holy Church, of the apostolic see, let him call him by his name, having first added the degree of his ministry, whatever it may be. But wherever the junior clergy meets him, he bows down and asks for a blessing from the senior; and if he finds a person sitting, let the younger one rise as he passes, and give him a place to sit, and let not the younger presume to sit down, unless his elder orders him to do so; that it may be done that which is written: Preceding one another with honor (Rom. 12).

Little children, or youths, in the oratory, or at the tables, with instruction, let them keep their orders.

CHAPTER III.-- *So that in those barriers all may sleep together.*

In this way we have arranged that the canonical clergy, who must live under the same order, God helping us, should all sleep in one dormitory, except those to whom the bishop has given permission, according to what seemed reasonable to him, to be in the very enclosures through the rooms arranged let them sleep separately; and they should each sleep individually, and in the same way they should sleep separately in the dormitory, mixed with the elders, for the sake of good foresight, so that the elders may foresee that the younger ones will act according to God. And no woman, nor lay man, shall enter the very gates, except only if the bishop, or archdeacon, or prefect has ordered it. In order that they may come to the refectory for the purpose of refreshment, they shall leave their weapons in front of the refectory, and as soon as they have left the refectory, they shall be led outside the bars; and if it be necessary for the work to be done, let lay men enter there; but when they have finished their work, let them go out with the utmost haste; and apart from the cause of necessity, if the clerical cooks are wanting, and the need arises, the lay cooks should only enter to cook; having finished their service, let them go out with speed.

And by those mansions the canonical clerics themselves should have no cleric of theirs without the precept of their bishop; and if he permits them to have it, let their conversation be such with humility and fear of God, that they displease neither God, nor the bishop, nor those who govern the assembly itself under their hand. And if they do otherwise, he who is in charge shall either excommunicate them, or let them receive corporal discipline. And neither cleric nor layman shall presume to drink, eat, or sleep in the very apartments within the very enclosures, except the clerics themselves who are in the congregation itself, or those clerics who serve their elders there in the enclosure itself by the order of their bishop. And whoever of the clergy has one cleric in the cloisters itself, as we have said, should provide for this, so that he has a plan with the rest of the clothes, and on Sundays, or other festivals, they stand dressed in their ranks in the church of God.

CHAPTER IV.-- *Of completor, or taciturnity.*

So that all the clergy who are in the assembly itself should come to the completionary, and at all times at the beginning of the night the first signal to the completionary should be sounded; and when at first that sign, which was ordained for this purpose, had been heard, let them immediately, wherever they were, come to their gates; and when they have heard the same sign again, let them all be in the church of St. Stephen, and then sing the complement in the name of God. And after they have sung the complement, they neither drink nor eat until the next day at the lawful hour; and let all keep silence, and let no one speak to another until the morning after the first has been sung, unless it be necessary, and this with the suppression of the voice with great caution, so that his voice may not be heard from that other dwelling which is near. and whoever among them has not been to the completion, after that night shall not presume to break down those doors, nor to enter through any place into the barriers themselves, before they come to the nocturnal. Neither the archdeacon, nor the first-in-command, nor that porter can give any provision from that point, so that someone may enter there after the completist, except for the nocturnal; except only if such a cause should occur, that it is necessary that that archdeacon, or the archdeacon, or whoever foresaw this at that time, should be able to tell that bishop for what reason this had been done; and if it be so that it is necessary, then they shall have leave to enter and to go out. And if it happens that it is necessary for the completist to report in the prisons for some reason, then let him come to that keeper of St. Stephen and make it clear to him, and he himself will report this in the prison. And if (which is far from happening) it should happen that any of the clergy who came before the completist in the city, or had previously been there, that if he had been daring or presumptuous, or negligent, persuading the devil, to stay some night somewhere in the city, except in his own barriers, if he does this once, if it is not done for a fault, he is reprimanded with words; and if the cleric himself repeats it, then on the same day it should be in bread and water; and if he does this the third time, let him be on bread and water for three days; and if he presumes to do this further, let him be subject to corporal discipline, so that the rest may fear him; and if, by persuading the devil, they delay anything by this, so that the completist does not come into the city before he has permission to be outside the prisons, and the bishop, or the archdeacon, or the prefect are able to investigate this, the cleric who committed this vice shall either be excommunicated, or subject to physical discipline.

CHAPTER V.-- *Of the divine offices at night.*

In the winter season, that is, from November to Easter, according to the consideration of reason, a greater pause will be made at midnight, and already those who have been disposed to rise for vigils; at the end of the night, let them say the verse, Kyrie eleison and the Sunday Prayer, and make an interval; with the exception of Sundays and saints' festivals, according to the consideration of the bishop, or those who are under him, that is, forty or fifty psalms may be sung by whoever orders this, or when he sees fit and the hour permits. And those who need a psaltery or a lesson, let them serve as meditation, and meditate in the same interval. let them make provisions; and he who does otherwise shall be excommunicated; all the rest should keep the order of vigils until the said mornings. At the first hour all in the church of St. Stephen sing the first.

CHAPTER VI.-- *That all the canonical hours should come to the divine service.*

At the hour of the divine office,so andn as the signal is heard, let all who have left whatever they have in their hands, who are so near to that house as they can meet there, come with the utmost haste; and if someone has been far from the church itself, so that he cannot attend to the work of God during the canonical hours, the archdeacon determines that it is so, and does the work of God with divine trembling wherever he is at the time; and let the archdeacon, or the first minister, or the custodian of the church, arrange that those signs sound at the appropriate hours.

CHAPTER VII.-- *On the discipline of playing*

We believe that there is a divine presence everywhere, and that the Lord's eyes watch the good and the bad; but above all let us believe this without any doubt, when we attend to the divine work; and therefore, we must always remember what the prophet said: Serve the Lord in fear, and rejoice in him with trembling (Psal. 2). And again: Psalter wisely (Psal. 46). And: In the presence of the angels I will sing to you (Psal. 137). For if we wish to suggest something to powerful men, we do not presume to do so except with humility and reverence; how much more must we supplicate to the Lord God of the universe with all humility and pure devotion? We took care of it in fear, according to what the Roman Church holds, and our synod has judged, that our clergy in the church, when assisting in the divine work, unless compelled by infirmity, should not hold staffs in their hands in the church.

CHAPTER VIII.-- *That they should come to the chapter every day.*

It is necessary that every day all the canonical clergy should come to the chapter, and there hear the words of God, and this institution of ours, which we have made for their benefit in order to save their souls, with the help of God, and each day they read some chapter from there; besides only on Sundays, and Wednesdays, and Fridays, treatises and other homilies, or whatever edifies the hearers, let them read to the chapter. For this reason, we decided to come every day to the chapter, so that both soul and soul may hear the word of God, and that the bishop, or archdeacon, or whoever seems to be in charge at the time, may order what he has to command, and correct what he needs to correct, or try to order what needs to be done. But the clerics themselves, when they go to the mansions after the first cantata, immediately hasten to prepare for themselves, so that when they hear the signal they may come to the chapter ready with speed; and all the clergy, who seem to be barricaded outside, and who are stationed in the city itself, should come to the chapter on every Sunday, prepared with plans, or official vestments, as the Roman Order has it. And on Sundays themselves, or on the celebrated feasts of the saints, let all the clergy, as we have said, who are outside the gates, come to the evening and morning hours, and on those days, keep their stations ready, so that each one may stand in his office until mass is finished; and if they have done otherwise, they shall be excommunicated by the archdeacon, or the superior, or even, if necessary, subject to corporal discipline. And on the Sundays themselves, as we have said, and on the celebrated feasts of the saints, let all be refreshed in the refectory with other clergy at the tables which have been arranged for them.

CHAPTER IX.-- *Of the daily work of the hands.*

Idleness is inimical to the soul: therefore, we decree that at the command of the bishop, or archdeacon, or prefect, or those who are ordained by them, the clergy should go forth from the chapter to the work where they are enjoined, and with a good heart, without murmuring, fulfill their obedience. and when it is not necessary to do common work, each one afterwards does what he has to do.

CHAPTER X.-- *Of those who set out on a journey.*

Those of the clergy who are on a journey with the bishop, or who set out elsewhere, must not neglect their order, as far as the journey or reason permits. And they must not pass the appointed hours, both for divine offices and for other purposes.

CHAPTER XI.-- *Of the good zeal which the servants of God ought to have.*

Just as the evil jealousy of bitterness separates from God and leads to hell, so is the good jealousy that separates from vice and leads to the Lord and eternal life. Therefore, let the servants of God exercise this zeal with the most fervent love, that is to say, that they anticipate one another with honor, and bear with the utmost patience their infirmities, whether of bodies or of manners; and if any vices are to be checked, or chastisement to be applied, let them agree in goodness with those to whom it is committed to see this, and God's helpers, as the apostle says, exist, how vices, if they have arisen, may be able to destroy them, to challenge each one to a better state, because it is written is: Those who love the Lord, hate evil (Ps. 25); for he who loves iniquity hates his own soul; for he loves his own soul well, who guards himself, and leads others to an example of good behavior both in words and deeds.

CHAPTER XII.-- *That one should not presume to kill or excommunicate the other.*

Every occasion of presumption is forbidden in this canonical order. although someone by his own presumption destroys him in this, either in words or in deeds, he is not to judge his own, but let him come to the former; let him define the cause itself according to the order; and he who presumes to do this shall be judged by the bishop, or by him who is under him.

CHAPTER XIII.-- *That in the gathering of clerics it is not permitted for one to defend the other.*

In every way it is necessary to be careful that one does not presume to defend another on any occasion, nor is it presumed by the canons, as if by obtaining kinship, or some kind of friendship, or familiarity, because a serious occasion for scandals in the congregation usually arises from this cause. But if anyone transgresses these things, let him be more strictly controlled, that the rest may have fear.

CHAPTER XIV.-- *On confessions.*

Scripture encourages us by saying: Reveal your way to the Lord and trust in him (Ps. 36). And again, he says: Confess to the Lord, because he is good, because his mercy endures forever (Ps. 55). And again, the prophet said: I have made my crime known to you, and I have not hidden my iniquities (Psal. 31). And again: I said, I will declare my iniquities against myself to the Lord; and thou hast forgiven the impiety of my sin (Ibid.); and again: Confess your sins to one another, that they may be blotted out (James 5); and elsewhere: He who conceals his crimes shall not be punished; but he who has confessed them has saved his soul from death (Prov. 28). And the Lord says in the Gospel: Repent, for the kingdom of heaven is near (Matthew 3). Therefore, it is necessary that while we have committed many things contrary to the will of God, or against the commandment of God, just by persuading the devil, we must make amends by true confession and true repentance, as the Scriptures teach. The Holy Fathers, who were perfect, decreed that at present, when any evil thought occurs in the heart of the servants of God, persuading the devil, they should immediately confess it to their predecessor by humble confession.

We mere lazy and frail people, although we do not follow their footsteps entirely, it is necessary that we should follow their footsteps in some part, according to which God has given us the possibility, so that through true confession we may deserve to have the kingdom of God. Thus, we have decided that our clergy should make their confessions to their bishop twice a year, at those times, one time at the beginning of Lent before Easter, and the other time from the middle of the month of August until Kalends. November: between these days, when the bishop has permission, and to whom it is necessary, he may make his confession at another time to the bishop, or to another priest to whom the bishop has decided to make it, whenever he wishes and has need. And those whose sins do not hinder them from the clergy on all Sundays and glorious festivals should receive the body and blood of our Lord Jesus Christ, because the Lord says in the Gospel: He who eats my flesh and drinks my blood remains in me and I in him (John 6) ; for if anyone has unworthily taken the sacred mysteries, he eats and drinks this judgment for himself (1 Cor. And if any of the clergy, who is absent, when he makes his confession to his bishop, is so filled with a diabolical spirit that he dares to conceal some of his sins from his bishop, and goes as if through other priests giving his confessions, and wants his bishop to hide his crimes , because he fears that the bishop may remove him from the rank, and if he is not yet in rank, he should not approach the rank, or promote him to the body of the Lord, or he should pursue those vices; If the bishop has been able to investigate this by any means, and it has been approved by him, let him suffer corporal discipline, or imprisonment, or anything else that the bishop sees fit, according to the manner of the guilt, so that others may fear and not fall into such a crime, because he is too unscrupulous. he sins before the eyes of God, and he is ashamed to confess to man, where, pitying God, he should receive counsel for healing from the sin itself.

CHAPTER XV.-- *Of graver faults.*

If any cleric of the canonical order commits graver sins, that is, murder, fornication, adultery, theft, or commits one of the principal vices similar to these, he must first be subject to corporal punishment; then how long does the bishop want, or those who are under him, to suffer imprisonment or exile, knowing that terrible sentence of the apostle who said: "Treat such a man to the destruction of the flesh, that the spirit may be saved in the day of the Lord" (1 Cor. 5). And while he is in the prison itself, none of the clergy shall join him in any company, nor in conversation, except to whom the prior has commanded, and alone persisting in penitential mourning as long as the prior has seen fit.

Having come out of prison, if it pleases the bishop, or those who are under him, he still performs public penance; that is, he should be suspended from the oratory at the same time as from mass, and at all the canonical hours he should come before the door of the church, where the prior had ordered everybody to lie prostrate before the very door of the church, until all had entered; there he did his duty as far as he could. On leaving the church, let him lie prostrate in the same way, until all have gone outside; and lying down, or standing before the very threshold, he speaks with no man.

As for abstinence, for as long or as it seems to the bishop, or those who are under him, in the measure or at the hour that he sees fit; nor should he be blessed by anyone until he is reconciled. He who, when called, comes to reconcile before the bishop or the clergy, prostrates himself with all humility from everybody on earth, and asks forgiveness from all, and the bishop will reconcile him according to the canonical order.

CHAPTER XVI.-- *Of those who are joined without judgment and excommunicated.*

If any brother presumes, without the order of the bishop, or those under him, to associate himself in any way with the excommunicated cleric, or to speak with him, or to direct him a command, or a letter, he shall be subject to the excommunication of vengeance.

CHAPTER XVII.-- *On the excommunication of bodies.*

If any cleric is obstinate, or disobedient, or proud, or drunken, or detractor, or contradictor, or rebellious, or contentious, or murmuring, or has transgressed the prescribed fast, or has disdained the command to stand at the cross, or has not asked for forgiveness when rebuked, or If, on the contrary, he is found to be contemptuous of this little institution and the precepts of the bishop, or of those who are under him, let him, according to the precept of our Lord, be admonished once and twice secretly by his elders; if he does not amend, he will be reprimanded publicly before all; but if he does not correct himself in this way, if he understands what the punishment is, let him be subject to excommunication; but if he is wicked, or less intelligent, or incorrigible, he is subject to corporal vengeance.

CHAPTER XVIII.-- *Of those who offend in some lesser matters.*

If anyone in the clergy comes late to the work of God, or to the table, or for some reason his elder has ordered him to sing psalms or masses, and he has not fulfilled this at all, and if he has broken something, or lost something, or has missed something else, and has not come immediately before the bishop, or those who are under him, he himself shall be satisfied on the other hand, and if he discloses his offence, while it is known by another, he shall be subject to a greater correction, according to the manner of the fault, as the bishop or those who are under him see fit; for if he himself confessed voluntarily, he should be subject to a lighter correction, as we have said, according to the nature of the guilt.

CHAPTER XIX.-- *What should be the manner of excommunication.*

According to the mode of fault of excommunication or discipline, the measure must be extended, which mode of fault depends on the judgment of the bishop, or those who are under him. For neither those who commit grievous sins, nor those who transgress in some light ones, are to be judged equally; but medicine must be used according to the disease, because neither a pious physician heals wounds, nor can he who refuses to take spiritual medicine obtain healing from spiritual medicine.

CHAPTER XX.-- *On the Fortieth Observations.*

Although the life of Christians should be simple and sober at all times, it behooves especially religious minds to live more constantly in these days and strive to cling to God in diligent service. And therefore, we decree that in those forty days before Easter, with all purity of mind and body, our clergy, commanding God, should keep themselves as far as they can. And concerning the perception of food and drink, in so far as God has given them help, let them be sparing; that is, that every day, with the exception of Sundays, from the beginning of Lent until the holy Passover, after the aforesaid evening they should always rest in repast; and let them abstain from those foods or drinks, as the bishop has determined with reason. And let them rest somewhere, neither in the city itself, nor in the monasteries, or in any places or houses belonging to them during these forty days, except perhaps, if he were far away, so that he could not be with his brethren at a competent hour to receive his food; then, because of that necessity, he should have permission to take such food as the rest of the clergy; and he should see to it that the competent hours do not precede him.

But for the reading the brethren in this Lent are free from the first saying until the third; and outside the gates, unless they go out only through those churches which are below the house, unless it is necessary, and the bishop, or one who is under him, has judged that what must be done is done. And after the third time they should have a chapter.

But from Passover until Pentecost they should fast twice a day, and they should have permission to eat flesh, unless they were penitents, except only on Fridays. From Pentecost until the birth of St. John the Baptist they should likewise eat twice a day and abstain from meat until the mass itself. But from the birth of St. John until the passing of St. Martin, so as before they should fast twice a day, and on Wednesdays and Fridays they should abstain from meat. From the passing of St. Martin until the Nativity of the Lord, let them all abstain from meat, and fast until the ninth on all these days, and eat in the refectory. After the Nativity of the Lord until the beginning of Lent, on Mondays, Wednesdays, and Fridays, let them eat in the refectory until the ninth day, and on the remaining days let them eat twice in the same refectory. But they should abstain from meat on Wednesdays and Fridays at these times. And if such a feast day should come in these two days, if the former permits, they shall eat the flesh.

On account of the infirmity of our clergy, we have considered that if on Wednesdays or Fridays, or at the other times, such as we have determined that they should abstain from meat, it is necessary, the bishop, or those who are under him, should have permission to consider their infirmities, or necessities, or festivals. to send, as he had foreseen that it would be well.

And it pleased me to be added to Anghilramn, the archbishop and chaplain of the most excellent King Charles, because while we and our clergy from Pentecost until the octaves of the second Easter, or the coming of the Holy Spirit, seem to celebrate with a devout mind, so that during these most sacred eight days the clergy of St. Stephen the protomartyr, or our let him have flesh to eat, except those who, for the saving of their souls and penance, have chosen to abstain.

CHAPTER XXI.-- *On the ordering of the month.*

The bishop's first table should be with guests and strangers, and the archdeacon, or those whom the bishop has commanded, should sit there. The second table with the elders. The third with the deacons. The fourth with the subdeacons. Fifth with the rest of the steps. Sixth with the abbots, or whom the prior commanded. On the seventh day, let the canonical clerics, who remain outside the gates in the city, rest on Sundays, or on great festivals. But when the hour for refectory comes, and the signal to the refectory is rung, then let the brethren arrive there with haste, and enter the refectory together, and pray together, and say the verse; and when the bishop, or another priest, has delivered the blessing over the tables, let all answer Amen; and as the order is arranged, let each one go to his own table.

But let the clergy maintain complete silence in the refectory, meanwhile they go out, how they can hear that divine lesson and meditate in their hearts. Because it is necessary that when it receives bodily food, and then the soul is refreshed with spiritual food. And the lector, and the cellarer, and the porter, or the weekman, or those who minister when the bishop and the clergy are making refreshments in the refectory, before the brethren come into the refectory, shall receive a mixture of bread and drink, so that it will not be a burden to them to endure the fast while the clergy are making refreshments. For the reader should read until the prior orders him to complete the reading.

It must be absolutely observed that neither priests, nor deacons, nor subdeacons, nor any of the clergy, carry food, nor anything else that pertains to eating or drinking, from the refectory without the order of the bishop.

And this must be taken care of, so that before the legitimate hour, except those who must provide for this, they must not enter the refectory either to eat or to drink without the order of the bishop, or whoever is in charge at that time, nor disturb the storeroom contrary to reason; but in competent hours they ask what is to be asked, and are given what is to be given.

But in the refectory itself, neither layman nor cleric, except those who are in the congregation itself, shall eat or drink, without the judgment of the bishop, or those who are under him. And in the cloister where the clergy come to the chapter, or in the refectory, none of the clerical servants who are there subject to their senior should enter, unless it is necessary, or the bishop, or those who are under him, have ordered it.

CHAPTER XXII.-- *On the measure of food.*

When our clergy refreshes twice a day at the appointed times, as it is written above, let them take enough bread. But the soup for the sixth. Let them receive one serving of meat between two, and one serving of food; and if they have no victuals, then let them have two servings of meat or bacon. At supper, let them have either one serving of meat between two, or one victual.

At that time when they must lead a life of Lent, then to the sixth between the two brothers they should receive a portion of the formate and food, and if they had fish, or vegetables, or something else, a third should be added. And at a meal between two, let them take one food, or a portion of a formate; and if God gives more, let them receive it with thanksgiving. But when there has been one repast in the day, then let them take one meal between two, and a portion of the formatico, and one serving of vegetables, or some other soup; and if it happens that in that year there is no grain or chaff, and they have no source from which it is permissible to fill the measure of meat afterwards, let the bishop provide according to which God has given the possibility, either from Lent, or from some other source, from which they can have consolation.

CHAPTER XXIII.-- *On the measure of drink.*

When it is to be eaten twice a day, the priests should take three cups for the sixth, and two for the supper; For deacons who are in rank, three for Friday, two for dinner, two for subdeacons for Friday, two for dinner. the rest of the steps, two for sixth, one for supper. But when there is one refreshment in the day, as formerly at the sixth hour, when they ate twice, let them take as many cups as possible; and that which they took of the drink at dinner, let this remain in the cellar; and let them avoid drunkenness altogether.

But if it happens that there is less wine, and the bishop cannot fill this measure, he must fill according to what prevails; but those brothers do not murmur, but give thanks to God, and endure with equanimity. For if it is possible for them to have so much, then by no means should it remain. And let the bishop, or whoever is under him, provide for those who abstain from wine, that they may have as much of beer as they ought to have of wine; and if the bishop wishes to add some drink to the measure above written, it shall be in his power, and he shall console them with beer. For when some refreshment comes for exigent reasons, we no longer agree to one refreshment, but to take the above-mentioned measure of three cups, and this seems superfluous to us, because wine causes even the wise to apostatize (Ecc. 19), because where there is drunkenness, there is debauchery and sin. it is. And we remind you that our clergy should lead a completely sober life; and since we cannot persuade them that they do not drink wine, or let us agree to this, that at least drunkenness should not dominate in them, because the Apostle declares that all drunkards are strangers to the kingdom of God, unless they repent by worthy penance.

CHAPTER XXIV.-- *Of the kitchen weeklies.*

Let the clerics and canons serve one another in such a way that no one is excused from the duty of the kitchen, unless he is ill, or is preoccupied with matters of serious utility, because from this a greater reward and charity is acquired. But consolations are to be procured for the weak, that they may not do this with sadness, but that all may have consolations according to the manner of the congregation, or the position of the place.

But the Archdeacon, and the Primicerius, or the cellarer, or those three guardians of the churches, one of St. Stephen, another of St. Peter, and the third of St. Mary, who are occupied with greater interests, these shall be excused from the kitchen; but the rest should serve one another under charity.

He is going out of the week on Saturday to do the cleaning; the vessels of his ministry, which he took to minister, he shall put back in the cellar, sound and clean, and if any of them has been diminished, he shall ask forgiveness of the chapter on the Sabbath, and restore the vessels, or whatever has been diminished, in its place, and according to which the bishop, or who is under it is by himself that he judges and repents.

CHAPTER XXV.-- *Of the archdeacon, or archdeacon.*

It is necessary for them to be wise as serpents and simple as doves, that is, to be wise for good and simple for evil. and learned the gospels and the canons instituted by the holy Fathers, that they might instruct the clergy in the divine law, and in this little institution. And in this way they conform themselves to the clergy, so that they may demonstrate the divine precepts not only with able words, but also by example, in simpler terms; those apostles must always keep the form in which he says: Argue, beseech, rebuke (1 Tim. iv); that is, mixing seasons with seasons, flattery with terrors, that is, they must rebuke the undisciplined and restless with more severity, but the obedient and meek and patient, they must entreat that they may progress better; but as soon as they begin to rise, they cut off the roots as they prevail, remembering the danger of Heli the priest of Shiloh, and rebuking them with more honest and intelligible words in the first and second admonitions; but let them beat the impious and hard-hearted and the proud or disobedient and check them with physical punishment at the very beginning of the sin, knowing that it is written: A fool is not corrected by words (Prov. 18); and again: Strike your son with a rod, and you will deliver his soul from death (Ibid.).

And whatever they have not been able to define justly and reasonably according to the canonical institution, or this small institution, let them make it completely clear to the bishop; and according to the will of God, he punishes what needs to be punished, and corrects what needs to be corrected. Those who are archdeacons, or chief priests, in all their acts or works must be faithful and obedient to God and the bishop, and must not be proud, rebellious, or contemptuous; but chaste and sober, patient, kind, and merciful, and mercy always exalts judgment, so that they may obtain the same. Let them love the clergy, hate their vices, but act prudently in the correction itself, and do nothing too much, lest, while they are desirous of eradicating the rust, the vessel should be broken; Remember not to break a broken pen. In which we do not say that they allow vices to be nurtured, but that they hasten to cut them off prudently and with charity. Let them beware lest, while they have preached to others, they themselves become reprobates, paying attention to that commandment of the Lord: And he that saw the mote in thy brother's eye, sawest not the beam in thine own; first cast out the beam from your own eye, and then you will see that you have removed the speck from your brother's eye (Matt. 7).

If the archdeacon, or the archdeacon, if they are found to be absent, proud, or proud, or contradictors, or despisers of the canon and of this small institution, let them be admonished once and again according to the Sunday precept; If they do not correct themselves in this way, let them be expelled from their ranks, and others who are worthy and have fulfilled the will of God or of their bishop according to the divine command, be substituted in their places.

CHAPTER XXVI.-- *Of the cellar*

But the steward must be God-fearing, sober, not drunken, not contentious, not hot-tempered, but modest, careful and faithful in his manners, and whatever he receives under his care for the work of the clergy he must faithfully keep, and without the judgment of his bishop, or who is under him. do nothing; and he must not be prodigal or exterminator of the substance of clerics, because if he is, without doubt he will give an account to God on the day of judgment; for if he has served well, he will acquire a good degree for himself.

CHAPTER XXVII.-- *Of the porter.*

One porter, together with his junior, should guard the gates, barriers, or doors for a year, or more, if it pleases the bishop. Let the porter be sober, patient, who knows how to receive an answer and to pay it back, and faithfully guard the gates, or doors of the prison, and do not presume to act contrary to this tenor, which if he does, he shall be excommunicated. But he shall return the keys of the gates to the archdeacon completist; and if the archdeacon is anywhere, let him who is under him receive the keys themselves.

But the custodians of the churches who sleep there, or are placed in the rooms nearby, should keep silence, like the rest of the clergy, as far as they can; and they shall not eat or drink behind the guard, and they shall not allow those who have remained outside the bars behind the guard to enter, nor those who are inside the bars to go out through the doors assigned to them. And if they have done so, they will be judged by the bishop, or by those who are under him.

CHAPTER XXVIII.-- *Concerning infirm canonical clerics, who have joined themselves more particularly to this order, and have no means of fulfilling their needs in their infirmity.*

If any of the clergy become infirm, who have joined themselves to this order in a more special way, and have not had wherewith to meet their needs in their infirmity, after the bishop the archdeacon and the chief minister shall take the greatest care of them, and they shall take care that the infirm are not neglected, but that they should be served as truly to Christ. . Because he himself said: I was weak, and you visited me; and as you did it to one of the least of these, you did it to me. Therefore, everything necessary, whatever is expedient and necessary for the sick, should be taken care of for them completely and without any delay, because he regards in them whatever they have had less of or have been neglected. And without a doubt, on the terrible day of judgment, when the King of the living and the dead will sit in the seat of his majesty, they will be given an account of all these, how they served them. And if the archdeacon himself, or the prefect, or the plenipotentiary, do not have where they can provide for their needs, let them make this known to the bishop, and he himself, according to the fear and love of God, will see to it that what is expedient for the sick themselves to have where they can provide for their needs.

For those who are infirm, there should be apartments appointed over them, reasonably arranged, suitable and suitable, where they can be, while they recover from their infirmities. And let one of the clergy be deputed, fearing God, who takes the utmost care of the sick themselves in all their needs, and has comfort, if need be, according to what the prior has established, so that the sick may be served without murmuring and neglect. And let him know that if he has served well, he will get a good degree for himself.

But even the weak should consider that they are served in the honor of God, and not grieve those who serve him by their own superfluity. They are only too weak to bear; but when they have improved, let them return to their ranks.

CHAPTER XXIX.-- *Of clerical clothing, shoes, or wood.*

That half of the clergy who have been elders should receive new caps every year, and always return the old ones they received last year, while they receive new ones. And the other half of the clergy should receive those old caps which those seniors pay every year, and those seniors should not exchange those caps which they must pay. Those priests who constantly serve there in the house, and those 7 deacons who stand in their rank, shall receive sheaves, or wool from which they have two sheaves in the year, and that other clergy each one. But those priests and deacons should receive two vestments each year. the subdeacon's shirt and a half, and those who are in the other degrees, individually. As for shoes, every clergyman should receive a pair of skins every year, four pairs only.

Regarding the wood, we have considered that the tenants of four pounds are able to procure wood sufficiently for a year; The very wood of those taxes, which are in the city or in the villages, should be procured for them, that is to say, four pounds shall be sent for this purpose. And Cal. May they receive the tax itself, and then buy the wood itself. And those caps, and those sackcloths, and those shoes, of those tolls mentioned above, which he then exceeds, and of that shoe, which that bishop was wont to pay every year to that clergy, and of their alms, which God specially gave to that clergy, let them be procured. And if there is anything from it, they procure something else that is necessary for them, or store it in their room. And if there they had not enough to provide for this, that bishop should provide for this and send, so that all this may be fulfilled for their need, as it is written above.

But let them receive the very clothes, those caps, and the sackcloth, for the passage of St. Martin; let them take those shirts twenty days after the Passover; those shoes Kal. They should have it in September. And if any one of the clergy of the church has received such a benefice from the bishop, that from it he can provide for his necessities, that is, caps and shoes.

CHAPTER XXX.-- *Of the festivals of the saints.*

He was pleased to intimate that we and our clergy should try to do that divine duty long and night, as far as God has given the possibility, to celebrate the festivals of the Lord, and of St. Mary, or of the twelve apostles, or of the rest of the saints, which he used to celebrate every year in that province. And the bishop, on the Nativity of the Lord, and the Lord's Passover, should make a repast for the clergy themselves in the house, if he is present, and if he is absent during these days, then let them have a sufficient repast in their refectory, as is written above. And after they had left the refectory, they drank two or three times in the chimneys, in order that they might be comforted, and that drunkenness should not prevail.

And the Epiphany of the Lord, and the middle of the Passover, and the close of the Passover, and the Ascension of the Lord, and Pentecost, and the birthdays of the bishop, on these days the bishop shall make them the sixth meal in the refectory. And with regard to those festivals, whence the abbeys in that city, or abroad, have, as they had the custom, to make refreshments for the clergy, this should not remain at all as far as was possible.

And that archdeacon, or whoever seems to be in charge at that time under the hand of the bishop, shall receive this, and the clergy shall then make refreshments in the refectory, and what is left shall be reserved for their work in the cellar. And that archdeacon, from his action, which he foresees for their work, the purification of Saint Mary, and of all the apostles, and of Saint John the Baptist, and of St. Remedies, let them have a repast at six in the refectory.

CHAPTER XXXI.-- *Regarding the fact that whoever wishes to associate himself with this special canonical order of this congregation, of the things he owns, makes a solemn donation to the church of the blessed Paul the Apostle by present; reserved, however, during the time of his life in the usufructuary order.*

It is true that we read that the ancient Church existed under the time of the apostles in such unity and harmony, and left everything in such a way, that everyone, selling his estates, laid the prices at the feet of the apostles, so that none of them dared to claim anything of his own, but all things were common to them. whence they were said to have one heart and one soul (Acts iv.); for every day breaking bread around the house, which was received in common by both men and women, or children, and all the common people, inflamed with the ardor of faith, and provoked in the love of religion, provided all with thanksgiving. but since it is not possible to be persuaded in our times, let us at least agree to this, that we may contract our minds to any resemblance of their behavior, because it is too inert, lukewarm, and lax in devotion, such that, as we have said, all the common people agreed in the name of God, we who are more particular to the canons we must serve the orders, however much we may not consent to this perfection. And if we cannot leave everything, let us keep it for our own use only, as we will not let it be released, not to our carnal heirs and parents, but to the Church, whom we serve in common under the authority of God, for whose affairs we have payments, instead of leaving it as an inheritance: so that, if with those who are perfect, for perfect abdication and contempt of this world, the crown is not given, or forgiveness of sins, as for the least, is granted by divine mercy. Because St. Prosper, or other holy Fathers, according to divine authority, have sanctioned that those clerics who wish to live on the affairs of the Church, may, by means of paper instruments, forgive the property they have, to God and the Church whom they serve, and thus use the affairs of the Church more freely without the greatest guilt. so that just as the clerics themselves rejoice over the affairs of the Church, so also the Church is congratulated on the affairs of the clergy themselves with their poor, thus increased and improved. Nevertheless, so that the clergy themselves, while they live, if it so pleases, may have their possessions in usufructuary order through the benefice of the church, so that all things may be common, and on account of their death they may return to the church, or to the canonical order to which they had previously been given. In the same way, pointing out that those clerics who have a sufficiency of their own resources should live on their own things, if they are nevertheless weak, so that they do not want to give in everything to the whole of the Church of God whom they serve, and thus spend the Church itself in the love of Christ with free servitude and diligent modulation ; and let them know that for this reason, because they use the things of the Church like the rest of the canons, they will receive special mercy from God, whom they serve out of their own things; because they also in a certain way leave their own, when they are content with their own things, and think that nothing should be received by them by right. But if they think therefore that a portion of what is given to the Church ought to be received, and not be seen to throw it away, because they cannot leave it to their own, because it would be indecent for them to be returned among their own poor, they should know that they would be more disfigured in possessing to feed the poor from the alms. For this must be taken care of, so that the mother Church is not burdened, which must be constantly devoted to the daily support of the poor, widows, and orphans, and at the same time the needy, constrained by the judgment of the canons.

Therefore, whoever wishes to associate himself with this canonical order, which we wish to restore in any way, as we have intimated in the little decree that we have said, and of the things he has solemnly donates by present to the church of blessed Paul for the work of God, or to the clerics who serve there. They return without any consignment or expected delivery. And let him be permitted to make alms for the poor, as well as for the congregation itself, and wherever he chooses, and fulfill his needs, out of all his movable property, as long as he lives and remains in the same order. And if any of his movables remained after his death, the half-part in alms to the poor, or his promises, or wherever he wished, to the archdeacon, or to the archdeacon, or to whom he himself, while living, begged the steward: and that half-part in his alms to the clergy. or to the congregation itself, let him return. And the clerics themselves have no power to reduce, or sell, or share in the very things which they have in their precariats, neither of the lands, nor of the vineyards, or forests, meadows, houses, buildings, mancipi, acolas, or any immovable things, except that We have said, let the living do what they will with the fruits of that, or what they have been able to work there.

But if it happens, persuading the devil, that one of these brothers, who have had very precarious things, falls into some grave or light crime, he should do penance according to what the bishop has judged him to do;

yet he ought not to be despoiled of the things which he possesses by precarious means for this purpose. And if any one of our abbots should desire to associate himself with foreign clerics in the same way as we have set up for this congregation above, he should do so in the same manner as the other brothers have done. But if there be another who wishes to associate himself with them, and to leave everything to the grace of complete perfection, let the bishop provide for them the necessities, how he may be able to fulfill the good work which, inspired by God, he began.

CHAPTER XXXII.-- *On almsgiving.*

Regarding the receiving of alms, we have established it in such a way that if anyone wishes to give something in alms to one of the priests for his mass, or for confession, or for infirmity, or for any of his charas, whether living or dead, the priest shall receive this from the giver, and thenceforth what he wills let him do If, however, he wishes to give something in alms to all the priests under such a condition, or in any other way, let this come to all the priests as well as to all the canons, and let all have this alms in common. Likewise, those alms which come in common to all the clergy, let them all have in common, and let them perform psalmody or masses for the alms themselves, as the bishop has instituted.

For this reason, we made a measure for the priests to receive alms for their own work, because we thought it would be too heavy a burden for them, if it happened to those priests alone to bear such enormous burdens of sinners. because it is easier for many to obtain God's mercy for sinners than one, however diligent; and everyone must fear for his own conscience, how much more for the sins of others, should he not heap upon himself a load of sins beyond his strength?

Let the archdeacon, or superior, receive these alms, and spend them in the necessities of the brethren, as they need them, and as the bishop has judged; and if there is anything left over from that, let them hide it in the wardrobes of the brothers.

CHAPTER XXXIII.-- *On Sundays, or on the feasts of the saints, how they should meet at the chapter or at mass.*

On Sundays, or on the feasts of the saints, or when the pontiff or those who are under him have commanded, in the morning after the first cant all should put on their official clothes, with their planets, as the ecclesiastical order has it, and they should be ready, and without delay they should meet with haste to the office. Now that the first sign has been heard, let all come to the chapter house, and, having heard the lesson, go under one to the church; and when the second signal is done, they sing the third, and, sitting in their ranks, wait for the pontiff, as is the custom of the Roman Church; and after that no one should leave his order, until he has fulfilled everything, except those who accompany the pontiff in obedience, or those who have been occupied in some interest, if it is such that he cannot be released at all, and let this be known to the bishop, or those who are under him . If any of the clergy of any order, whether priests, or deacons, or subdeacons, or acolytes, were not present at that time ready to fulfill their duty, and any neglect or retardation should happen by him, except by reason of grave infirmity, on the morrow from wine or he is deprived of drink; But if, through laziness or contempt, he repeats himself, let him be checked more vigorously by the bishop, or by those who are under him, so that the rest may have fear. For the rest of the days, they should come to the chapter, as we have indicated above in this tenor.

But if there is a public station in those forecourt churches, and the brethren have celebrated a vigil there, when the vigil is over, they should return to the prisons in the morning with all decorum, so that they may come completely to the chapter; If, however, he delayed negligently, and was not at the chapter, he shall be punished for this the first and second time. But if he does not make amends, on that day when he does not come to the chapter, let him abstain from wine until the next day.

CHAPTER XXXIV.-- *Of matriculants, that they should come to hear the divine lesson in the established church in the house.*

While we were writing about correcting the life of canonical clerics with necessary things, as it seemed to us according to our mediocrity and the capacity of sense through the help of God, we went to the matriculators both at home and in the suburbs, because it was not, according to the institution of the ancient Church, their conversation, but under they were placed in a kind of security, in great danger, and negligence, and, as I might say, without preaching and confession, they did not come to the house to the public station to hear the word of God, nor to the other stations, but they were all sitting, each one in his place. Therefore, together with the agreement of the spiritual brothers, we have decided that twice a month during the whole year from fourteen to fourteen days on the Sabbath all matriculants, both those who are in the house and those who have matriculations through other churches below the city or villages, all come to the established assembly in the church in the house , early in the morning waiting in their ranks, until the signal struck at three o'clock; then the coming bishop, if he has not been occupied with other interests, and orders him to read a lesson from the treatises, or appropriate homilies of the holy Fathers, which will edify the hearers and teach them the way of salvation, how they can reach eternal life with the help of God.

Said thirdly, if the bishop does not come, then the guardian priest of the church of St. Stephen will take his turns according to his capacity and read and teach them the way of salvation, and the presbyter will see that at the appointed hour, if the bishop does not come there, he will not pass by to fulfill this, because it is written here; and the matriculants themselves should make their confessions to the priest twice a year, once in Lent, another time in the mass of St. Remedies until the passage of St. Martin. And if, by the suggestion of the devil, some vices have arisen among them, scandals have arisen, so that it is necessary for him who has committed this to give his confession in the next assembly, where they hear the lesson; when the reading is over, let him make his confession cleanly to the priest himself; and if he himself does not want to confess his sin, and has concealed it, and if it has been discovered by another, he who conceals the offense shall either be excommunicated by the priest who proclaims the word of God to them, according to the manner of guilt, or subjected to corporal vengeance. And through each matriarch there should be a leader of the matriarchs who acts curiously upon them; and if any one of them wishes to conceal his crimes, and one of their foremost was able to investigate this, let him in no way conceal it from the priest who reads the lesson to them; and if he does the same, he who has committed this is to be judged by the priest himself; and if the presbyter himself was not able to correct this by himself, let him inform the archdeacon or the superior, so that they may correct this reasonably according to the nature of the fault; and if need be, let it come to the notice of the bishop, that he himself may amend this.

As we have said, let all matriculants come to the lesson on the appointed days, and let them reveal their needs, both of soul and body, to the presbyter; and he himself shall either amend this by himself, or let his predecessors know [...] And if any remain among the matriculants themselves, who does not come to the lesson, unless compelled by infirmity, he shall be reprimanded once and a second time, and if he does not amend, he shall be excommunicated; and if he does this further out of contempt, let him be cast out of the matron's house, and another who will hear the word of God be sent in his place. And we decreed that they should receive from the house as alms for us, or for our successors, every time when they came to hear that lesson, every one of them a loaf of bread, and a portion of the bacon at one time, and at another time a portion of the formate, to do so throughout the whole year. As we have said, those who came there from the matriculations themselves; and in Lent let them take two quarts of wine with bread, one pint out of four. At the Lord's Supper let them take the wine with the above-mentioned measure of bread, and a portion of lard, and of formate. And we have considered that eight measures of baked bread should be used for each turn; and that time when they should receive bacon, let them receive six bacons, and when they receive formate in each time one pound. He collects 200 bushels of corn per year from that corn that comes from Warmacinse, and he takes it when he comes from there. Let Kal take 60 bacons of the bacon. January, from the formatic, let him receive 12 pensas at the mass of St. Martin himself. The mass of St. Martin himself should receive 24 measures of wine. And let the archdeacon, or superior, receive all this, and let them see that they administer it in this way, as it pleases God, and we have an arrangement. And our wages, or those of our successors, or those who do this, should decrease from that point on, and to procure the wood from which they can make the bread itself, the bishop will give two and a half ounces of the denarii in the month of May. And if he has anything in excess of what we have said above, let him give it to other poor people, to whom it is necessary, the archbishop, or the chief minister, or to whom they have commanded.

The Scriptorium Project is the work of a small group of lay people of various apostolic churches who are interested in the preservation, transmission, and translation of the works of the early and medieval church. Our efforts are to make the works of the church fathers accessible to anyone who might have an interest in Christian antiquities and the theological, philosophical, and moral writings that have become the bedrock of Western Civilization.

To-date, our releases have pulled from the Greek, Syriac, Georgian, Latin, Celtic, Ethiopian, and Coptic traditions of Christianity, and have been pulled from sundry local traditions and languages.

Other Selections from the Early Frankish Church Series:

Frankish & Visigothic Councils: 549-615 AD (June 2007)
The Writings of St. Chrodegang of Metz by St. Chrodegang of Metz (Apr. 2010)
Letter to Brunhilda of Austrasia by St. Germain of Paris (Sept. 2010)
The Spiritual Combat by St. Bernard of Clairvaux (Dec. 2010)
In Praise of the New Chivalry by St. Bernard of Clairvaux (Jan. 2011)
Testament by St. Burgundofara the Abbess (Jan. 2016)
Laws of the Monastery and the Church by Theuderic III, King of Franks (Feb. 2016)
The Life of King Sigebert II by Sigebert of Gembloux (Mar. 2016)
Two Letters from a Gallic Patrician by Dynamius the Patrician (July 2016)
Life of St. Germain by St. Venantius Fortunatus (Aug. 2016)
Three Letters from the Companion of the Bulgars by St. Rupert of Juvavum (Aug. 2017)
An Account of the Gallican Liturgy by St. Germain of Paris (June 2018)
Preludes by Photius of Paris (Nov. 2018)
The Privileges of Rome by Louis I the Pious, Frankish Emperor (Apr. 2019)
Edicts of the Synod of Paris by Chlothar II, King of Franks (Aug. 2019)
Laws of the Church (Ecclesiasticae Praeceptiones) by Chlothar III, King of Franks (Apr. 2020)
Laws of the Church (Ecclesiasticae Praeceptiones) by St. Dagobert II, King of Franks (Sept. 2020)
Letters of Paulinus by St. Paulinus of Aquileia (Aug. 2021)
The Italian Diplomas by Charlemagne, Holy Roman Emperor (Apr. 2023)

www.ingramcontent.com/pod-product-compliance
Lightning Source LLC
LaVergne TN
LVHW061042070526
838201LV00073B/5147